RICH TIP$

FOR A

Lifetime

RICH TIP$

FOR A

Lifetime

HOW TO ACHIEVE SPIRITUAL,
EMOTIONAL, AND FINANCIAL
WEALTH 365 DAYS A YEAR

REBECCA SCOTT YOUNG, MBA

TWO HARBORS PRESS *Minneapolis*

Two Harbors Press
212 3rd Avenue North, Suite 290
Minneapolis, MN 55401
612.455.2293
www.TwoHarborsPress.com

ISBN-13: 978-1-937293-81-9
LCCN: 2011942121

Distributed by Itasca Books

Book Design by Kristeen Wegner

Printed in the United States of America

My entire family has been a continuous source of wisdom and encouragement. From my youthful days at my father's church to the many stages of my financial career, I thank everyone involved with this blessed journey called life.

I dedicate this book to all of those whom God sent
to make this journey so enjoyable.

CONTENTS

INTRODUCTION

"I want to be rich, I have all this debt, I want to buy [fill in the blank], I need to go shopping . . ." We have all said or thought these contradictions before. If you want to be rich, then you cannot blow your money. If you have a lot of debt, then why create more?

In *Rich Tips for a Lifetime*, you will not learn a "get rich quick" scheme. However, you will learn tips on how to make what you already have go further, how to get more for less, how to safeguard your financial future, and how to achieve Black Friday 365 days a year.

All purchases—big or small—affect your wallet. Yet many financial advisors do not sufficiently convey the impact that everyday purchases can have on your natural and financial well-being. In the pages ahead you will learn practical, simple tips on how to create a financially fit future, no matter the state of your current financial health.

Management with an emphasis on human resources has always been my ultimate career goal. Human resource management is simply a way to ensure effective and efficient use of human talents while achieving an organization's common goal. What interests me most about the field is that it promotes equality, diversity, and the optimization of an individual's performance.

Earning my bachelor of science degree in accounting from DeVry University in Pomona, California, and my master's of business administration degree in human resource management from La Sierra University in Riverside has allowed me to excel in the financial arena and establish my own financial house. Along with these degrees, I have also earned my Series 6 and 63 financial services licenses. These allow me to act as a representative to sell select financial products and give me the credentials necessary to conduct various financial transactions for clientele; they also allow me to educate families on financial independence and to establish their financial portfolios based on their identified financial and retirement goals. I have also educated families by holding seminars to teach basic financial concepts on saving and investing. This book contains the basic tips that I have shared with many other families so that they could achieve their personal and financial goals. Start nourishing your financial health today, and you too can be on your way to a financially fit tomorrow!

For over twelve years I have been employed as a senior internal accountant/auditor with my local county government and have worked intermittently with an investment firm as a manager and senior investment advisor. As a senior internal accountant/auditor, I have determined through complex audits how departmental accounting management programs should be structured and have made recommendations on how accounting principles should be applied. Working in the auditing and accounting field has taught me how to find answers, a skill I apply when answering clientele concerns. I gather the information, research the best options, and present the information to the individuals.

In addition, I have managed my own financial and tax services business. About ten years ago, I began preparing my own tax returns because I felt like my returns were not being prepared properly. Additionally, I figured I should be preparing my own tax returns since I was an accountant. Subsequently, family and friends wanted me to prepare their tax returns as well. That's when I decided to start my own small tax business.

In the past few years, my career goals have been defined and refined as my professional responsibilities have changed. As the years go by, I value my decision to complete my postgraduate degree all the more—it sets me apart from other individuals in the industry. I am currently working on my doctorate with an emphasis in entrepreneurship and business management at California InterContinental University in Diamond Bar, California.

While monetary rewards are of practical importance, true life satisfaction springs from the opportunity to grow and learn from every God-given experience. I look forward to the challenge and reward of educating my readers, while sharing my life experiences along the way.

Shopping

At what point during the year do consumers stand in long lines, for hours at a time, in the cold, in hopes of purchasing one of three Blue Light Specials? You got it: Black Friday! Why not get those same deals, plus some, anytime you want? In today's economy, we are all trying to stretch our dollars; therefore, it is important to know what to do to make our money go further and to get more for less.

Over the years, I have been ripped off and it has angered me every single time. My breaking point occurred when I traded in a car to buy another one, and was given $6,000 less than its Blue Book value; the dealer turned around and sold my trade-in the next day for $12,000 more than I had been paid. I vowed never to allow a salesman to take advantage of me again, and from then on, I researched all my transactions before making them. The more prepared you are will reduce possible exploitation.

VALUABLE INFORMATION

- Do not let your shopping plan you. Plan for what you want to buy. If you are planning to purchase a new pair of shoes, research the local ads and download or clip the applicable coupons before making your purchase.

- Give yourself a spending budget and follow that set budget without exception. (I will expand on how to budget in the next chapter.)

- If it is hard to follow your budget, then leave your credit cards at home and only take cash. For example, if your budget is $80, then only take $80 to spend and leave the rest at home.

- Before leaving the house to shop at a specific store, search the Internet for coupons using the following sites:

  www.couponcabin.com
  www.dealigg.com
  www.couponmountain.com
  www.dealtaker.com
  www.shopathome.com
  www.retailmenot.com

If you are shopping online, you can use these sites to locate coupons or promotional codes that will discount your online purchases.

- Shop windows. Whether you have access to Windows 2000, Internet Explorer Windows, or the Windows on your phone application, use them. You will save money in the long run. For my purchases, whether in-store or online, I always use a search engine to browse for coupons. For example, if I'm planning on going to Bath & Body Works, I would type in "Bath & Body Works printable coupons." From there, I would click on the applicable coupons, print them out, and take them with me to the store, or use the promotional code online. Often in my searches I find coupons for free items or those that save me dollar amounts off of my bill. It pays to be prepared.

- A big no-no is window shopping. Do not roam aimlessly in the mall, shopping center, or store without a clear agenda. Nine times out of ten you will pay too much for an item that could have been purchased for less or that you didn't even need in the first place. You must shop with a purpose. Be conscious of why you are going to the store, identify the item(s) that you are going to purchase, and stay within your set budget.

Consider ways you can improve your shopping habits. Write your ideas down here.

_____

_____

_____

_____

_____

_____

_____

_____

_____

_____

_____

_____

_____

_____

_____

_____

Budgeting

Everyone has different priorities when it comes to money management. However, the common denominator is formulating a budget. Doing so will help you cut out unnecessary expenditures and stay within your set limits.

HOW TO CREATE A BUDGET

- Calculate your monthly income.

- Make a list of your monthly expenses. This will help you identify budgeted items that may not be necessary.

- Establish a realistic timeline in which you will pay off all debts. For example, you might establish that you will pay off all your credit card debt in three years, with the added goal of paying off the card with the highest interest rate first.

- Determine how much you can save on a consistent basis.

- Set up automatic deposits for your savings account(s). Having various savings accounts for different purposes can be very beneficial. For example, you could set up a Christmas savings account, a vacation savings account, and a retirement savings account. In addition, you should always have savings set aside for a rainy day.

- Pay attention to wasteful spending. If you have a gym membership that you barely use, cancel it and save that money instead.

- Avoid the costs of eating out by preparing meals in advance.

- Cut up your credit cards, especially if you have several credit cards that are maxed out. I recommend keeping one credit card in case you need it for emergency purposes.

- Reduce the number of social gatherings you attend. Fifty dollars spent at each happy hour can add up quickly.

TIPS ON MAINTAINING YOUR BUDGET

When you create a budget and stay within your budget, you allow yourself to reach your personal goals.

- Be disciplined. Do not give into temptation when considering "must-have" items.

- Write out your grocery list to avoid impulse buys and purchase in bulk when possible.

Create your own budget using the steps we've just discussed. Which items are essential? Which would you consider wasteful spending?

_____

_____

_____

_____

_____

_____

_____

_____

Consider ways you can improve your monthly budget. List your ideas here.

_____

_____

_____

_____

_____

_____

_____

_____

_____

_____

_____

_____

_____

_____

_____

Groceries

Before you go to the grocery store, write down the items you need. This way you do not leave with unnecessary purchases or forget the items that you originally meant to buy. The following are some basic tips to help you save money on groceries:

- Browse your local ads for current sales.

- Clip or download coupons on items you plan to buy.

- Take advantage of discount stores. You can save on everyday items like paper goods, bath supplies, and even fruits and vegetables depending on your local area.

- Do not shop at overpriced grocery stores for the sake of convenience.

- Pay attention to prices. Compare prices where possible; for example, at your local grocery and convenience stores.

- If you are a single person and spend $100–$200 at the grocery store a week and still find yourself going back for more items, then you probably need to reevaluate what you are purchasing and where you are purchasing it. Of course, everyone is different, and the circumstances will change depending on your family size; however, the principle is still the same. Be conscious of every purchase.

MY STORY

One of my coworkers encouraged me to try a local grocery store in my area called Wincos. She said that the prices were really low and gave me a comparison of the cost of yogurt; when I finally went myself, I couldn't believe just how low their prices were. I typically spent around $250 on groceries every two to three weeks. However, I went to my local Wincos and spent $160 on almost a month's worth of groceries! I was floored.

The bottom line? Do your homework, pay attention to prices, and be conscious of what you typically spend. The money you save could be used towards achieving your saving and investing goals.

Write down steps you can take to achieve your savings goal.

_____

_____

_____

_____

_____

_____

_____

_____

_____

_____

_____

_____

_____

_____

Saving & Investing

To achieve financial independence, aside from reducing our spending and shopping habits, we have to save and invest. No one ever says, "I want to work all my life just to make ends meet!" More often, people say "I want to retire early" or "I want to be rich when I grow up or by the time I retire." I have even heard some of my friends say, "I want to marry rich so I don't have to work so hard anymore."

No matter a person's age, gender, race, profession, or income level, everyone needs to save for their future. You may say, "I barely have enough money to get by now; I'm not in a position to save any money." However, consider what would happen if you received an unexpected pay cut, perhaps as part of your company's effort to circumvent layoffs. Funds would be tight, but you would find ways to adjust. Maybe you'd have to reduce your phone plan or pass up on a few social gatherings; maybe you'd have to wash your own car.

Now, I say this not to disregard your financial situation, but to make the point that when changes are forced upon us, we adjust. We are all in a position to save money regardless of our financial situation; the key is to assess our individual circumstances and look for opportunities to save.

Question: How much money does the average person save for retirement? How much money does the average person save for emergencies?

Answer: The answer to both is "not enough." I recently read on *Bankrate.com* that two-thirds of Americans do not save enough money, especially when it comes to building a comfortable retirement.

Rule of Thumb: As a whole, save, at minimum, ten percent of every dollar that you make.

"He who gathers money little by little makes it grow."

—Proverbs 13:11

The amount of money that you need to save up for retirement varies depending on your current age, when you want to retire, and how much money you will need on a monthly basis. However, the sooner you start saving, the better off you will be. To obtain accurate figures, use one of the many savings or retirement calculators online; a few are suggested below. These calculators will give you real figures to confirm whether you are saving enough money to reach your personal financial goals.

Valuable Information

Here are a few useful websites to help you organize your finances in preparation for retirement:

- www.ingyournumber.com
- finance.yahoo.com/retirement
- retirement.ingdirect.com
- www.bankrate.com

You don't have to be a rocket scientist to retire comfortably. Just use the resources available to make your money work for you instead of working so hard for the money.

Once you calculate your numbers, set up an automatic savings plan that will invest and save the money for you. Some useful investment vehicles include:

- Your company's 401(k), Deferred Compensation Plan, or 403(b), if available. A 401(k) plan is an employer-sponsored plan where employees voluntarily elect to contribute a percentage of their annual salary. A 403(b) is a tax-sheltered annuity and works similarly to a 401(k). A tax-sheltered annuity is a retirement investment vehicle that allows you to make pre-taxed contributions.

- Sharebuilder.com – is a site that allows you to easily purchase stocks and to establish and maintain an investment portfolio. This site also offers a lot of free guidance regarding stocks, mutual funds, and investments that I have personally found very helpful and useful.

- Variable or equity universal life policy – are life insurance policies that builds cash value, where the cash value is then invested into a variety of separate accounts; these work similarly to how mutual funds work.

- CD or money market accounts – are conservative investment vehicles that are used to keep your money safe while earning a low interest rate return. CDs are short-term bank notes with a stipulated interest rate. Money market accounts are generally open-ended mutual funds that consist of low risk securities.

While these are all great options, it's best to contact a financial planner or go to your local bank to obtain more information, especially if investing is unfamiliar territory for you.

When it comes to saving for emergencies, it is best to have at least three times your monthly income stored away. Why? Well, if an unplanned event occurs, like your car needs a new set of brakes or tires, or your child needs new shoes or braces, you can make these necessary purchases comfortably. If you were to unexpectedly lose your job— a common consequence of the economy these days—your three months' worth of savings would buy you some time and pay your monthly obligations while you seek out new employment. When you have money set aside for those unforeseen events, it is one less thing you have to worry about.

This three-month emergency fund is in addition to the ten percent of your income that I suggested you save on a monthly basis. The emergency savings fund is monies that are set aside strictly for emergencies. While the three-month allotment is the suggested amount, it's always good if you can save more.

CREDIT CARDS

Another key to successfully saving is to avoid credit cards. Credit cards are not free money. You have to pay the credit card companies back for the money that you borrowed, in addition to the fees and the high interest rates that accumulate on a monthly basis. On average, credit cards—especially those given out by department stores—have interest rates at around twenty-four percent. Some credit card companies charge an additional fee, either monthly and/ or annually, just for having the credit card account opened. All these fees and interest charges have to be paid back on top of the cost of your initial purchases.

When Is It Okay to Close a Credit Card?

Many experts believe canceling or closing a credit card is generally not a good practice because doing so decreases your credit score and lowers the amount of credit available to you. Instead, these experts suggest that you keep the account open and shred up the card; this way the available credit line will appear on your credit report. That may be a good idea, but if you find yourself reordering another card or using your memorized credit card number for online transactions, you may need to take a more proactive approach.

Here are three situations in which I would advise you to close your credit card account:

1.   Your card has an extremely high interest rate, like between fourteen and twenty-four percent.
2.   You have too many cards and need to cut back on your spending. One card will serve its purpose and will help keep your spending under control.
3.   You are tempted to overspend.

Rule of Thumb: When deciding whether to put an item on your charge card, consider this: If you cannot pay off the purchase within thirty days, do not make the purchase. Instead, save up your money until you have enough cash to buy your desired item. This requires patience, but in return you do not have to worry about wasting money on extra charges or interest fees that the credit cards would incur.

MY STORY

A minimum of ten percent of each paycheck I receive is directly deposited into a separate savings account. I do this to prevent the temptation to use that money, which would otherwise appear available in my regular checking account. After purchasing the necessities each month, I put a percentage of the remaining funds into my savings account as well.

Over the years, I've learned that it is not necessary to spend all the money available in my checking account and that it is beneficial to save more when I am able to. It took me a while to reach this turning point in my finances, and clearly I'm not alone. Consider tax season, for example. Many individuals rush to file their income taxes so that they can buy a big-screen TV or a new wardrobe; most do not rush to file their taxes just so they can increase the size of their savings account.

> *Instead of feeling obligated or compelled to spend, tell yourself, "I am able to save my money. I will not make this unnecessary purchase." These little life changes can go a long way.*

Write down steps you can take to change your own spending habits.

_____

_____

_____

_____

Complete Financial Checkup

To ensure total financial health, here are the main topics you should explore with a financial consultant:

- Insurance: Assess your family's need and review existing policies.
- Retirement planning: Determine how much you will need to retire comfortably.
- Estate planning: Develop a will with financial and medical directives. A will simply explains how you want your finances handled and how you want your family and the doctors to address any given medical situation should you become incapacitated.
- Savings: Identify if you are saving enough to accomplish your own personal goals.

Review your finances and write down areas that may need a checkup.

_____

_____

_____

_____

_____

SAVINGS & INVESTING 101

In this section, I will give you an overview of saving and investing options and identify some of the retirement vehicles available to you.

What Should I Do with the Money I Save?

Mutual Funds

A lot of people look for innovative ways to make money and create wealth through tools like mutual funds, which are simply professionally managed investment accounts. However, mutual funds will not create an abundance of wealth.

Many case studies have been conducted to examine the financial habits of the wealthy and the conclusions are clear: the greater the net wealth, the smaller the percentage that is invested in mutual funds. The extremely wealthy (defined as those with a net worth over $10 million) have less than 5 percent of their wealth in mutual funds; the wealthy (those with a net worth between $1 million and $10 million) have only a slightly higher percentage of wealth in mutual funds. But the mass affluent (those with a net worth of $100,000 to $1 million) have close to 30 percent of their wealth in mutual funds. However, the mass of the general population, where most make $100,000 or less, invest a bulk of their wealth in mutual funds, if they are investing at all.

The reason for this discrepancy is that the rate of return on mutual funds has been below market, averaging 8–10 percent over the past ten years, as opposed to gain-ing returns averaging over 12 percent for more aggressive investment vehicles. Additionally, many people do not consistently invest in their mutual funds on a regular basis, against the instructions of their tax or financial advisor. Don't get me wrong—mutual funds are a good supplemental investment strategy; however, they should not be your only vehicle for generating a return.

Life Insurance

Life insurance provides unique benefits compared to other financial planning tools. Although the primary benefit of life insurance is that it provides cash upon the passing of the policyholder, it can serve as the family's emergency fund, as well as provide:

- Final expenses
- Dream fulfillment
- Spousal income
- Estate planning services

If others are financially dependent on you, life insurance is especially important as it will take care of your loved ones' immediate needs should you no longer be able to provide for them. Below is a list of the different types of life insurance available:

- Term insurance
- Permanent insurance
- Whole life insurance

- Universal life insurance
- Variable universal life insurance (VUL)
- Equity indexed universal life insurance (EIUL)

Based on my experience, the two most popular types of insurances are VUL and EIUL. The riskier of the two, VUL is an investment vehicle that has more growth potential since it is tied to the waves of the stock market. Thanks to the evolving economy, the last few years have resulted in a new approach to permanent life insurance, which takes the form of EIUL. The major difference with an EIUL policy is that you have the liberty to participate indirectly in the upward movement of a stock index without the normal risk associated with investing in the stock market. Therefore, if the stock market is favorable, you gain, but if it loses, you are not subject to the risk of lost money.

When reviewing your options, it is important to contact a tax or financial advisor to ensure you invest wisely according to your financial goals.

IRAs and Retirement Plans

Many financial planners recommend that you budget 80–85 percent of your annual salary just to maintain your current standard of living. But what about the appropriate savings plan to build a nice nest egg? Here are a few of the retirement savings options that can be designed to meet your individual needs:

- 401(k) – A 401(k) is an employer-sponsored retirement plan in which the employee decides the contribution amount and in many cases the employer may match up to a certain percentage.

- 403(b) – A 403(b) is a tax-sheltered annuity and works similarly to a 401(k).

- Profit sharing – is a company's designated percentage of annual profits that is shared with its employees.

- Rollover IRA – is a transfer of funds from an existing employer-sponsored account into a regular IRA account.

- Roth IRA – is a special retirement account that is generally not taxed.

- Simplified Employee Pension (SEP) IRA – is a self-employed retirement plan.

- Savings Incentive Match Plan for Employees (SIMPLE) IRA – is a tax-deferred employer-provided retirement plan.

- Traditional IRA – is an account that allows you to invest pre-taxed income towards investments that can grow tax deferred.

Tax deferral programs such as 401(k)s and IRAs were designed by the government for two reasons: They encourage folks to save money and increase tax revenues. By granting participants a tax break when money is put in and taxing any funds that are then taken out, the government is assured greater tax revenue based on even a meager rate of return.

It should be noted that these deferral options were never expected to be the only retirement vehicles, but an addition to the benefit pensions that were the norm at the time these programs were created. Over the last few decades, 401(k)s and IRAs have become the primary retirement vehicles that most people have outside of social security. And social security does not appear promising. According to www.SSA.gov (May 2011), recent studies indicated that social security benefits will be exhausted by 2036.

Creating Income

Do you find yourself thinking, *I need to make more money*? Well then, let's make more money. The following are some tips to consider:

- Ask for a raise. The following sites can help:

  www.careerplanning.about.com
  www.ask-for-a-raise.com
  www.payscale.com

- Seek out promotional opportunities within your organization.

- Create passive income. Passive income is income that you earn on a regular basis with little effort needed to maintain it. One option would be to invest in mutual funds, shares, or stocks and reinvest the gains. Check out the links below for more ideas:

www.redeemingriches.com
www.createpassiveincome.net
www.ameraco.com

• Consider what you love to do and find a way to earn revenue. If you love to take pictures, for example, you could become a part-time photographer. If you play an instrument, you could play at various venues for monetary gain. My father plays the piano and organ very well, and over the years various churches have hired him to play at special events.

• Using the skills you already have, create a small or part-time business. If you are affluent in another language, you could open a translation or tutoring business. If you enjoy watching children, you could become a babysitter. These small businesses allow you flexibility even if you have a full-time job; you can build your client base around your schedule. You just have to get your creative juices flowing and figure out what is best for you.

- If you have a vacant room and don't mind sharing your home with someone else, create rental income. If you are fortunate enough to own another property, consider renting it out to cover the mortgage expense. These are both examples of creating passive income.

- Sell items that you no longer use, or even artwork that you have created.

MY STORY

By trade I am an accountant. However, I have a small tax and financial services business that I run out of my home. I offer year-round tax preparation services, notarize documents, and provide financial consulting services by appointment only. I have also created a diversified portfolio for myself and for my family. For example, I have the following in my portfolio: a deferred compensation plan, mutual funds, stocks using the ING ShareBuilder program, savings accounts, a variable universal life policy, and an equity indexed universal life policy. It is important to diversify your investments and not put all your eggs in one basket. Since asset values generally do not move up and down simultaneously, having a diversified portfolio will reduce your level of investment risk.

Additionally, a couple of years ago I used a real estate property locator program, where I gained $10,000 on one of my first transactions. This was a program that assisted with the acquisition and liquidation of distressed properties. As a property locator, I had to locate the distressed properties and connect the investors with the distressed property owners. I did not have to earn a real estate license or take any tests. To create additional income, I have also done occasional modeling and have acted as a movie extra.

There are a vast number of ways you can make additional income. Here is a plan of action to help you get started.

- First, think about what you want to do and what you want to accomplish. Identify your goals. Perhaps you want to become a real estate agent, seek a promotion at your job, or ask for a raise. Write down your ideas.

- Make a plan for how you will accomplish your goal. For example, if your goal is to become a notary, you will have to take the course, pass the test, obtain your bond and the necessary materials, create business cards, and market yourself.

- Do not be your own worst critic. Avoid negative thinking and turn obstacles into opportunities.

- Encourage yourself—you can accomplish anything.

- Once you begin, the pieces will come together.

- Believe!

> *"Careful planning puts you ahead in the long run;*
> *hurry and scurry puts you further behind."*
>
> —*Proverbs 21:5*

You'll be amazed how much further you can go in life by simply taking a few minutes at the beginning of each day to set your thoughts in the right direction.

> *Plan to be successful and do something daily to feed that plan.*

Think of ways you can create passive income and list your ideas here:

_____

_____

_____

_____

_____

_____

_____

Describe how you will accomplish these goals:

_____

_____

_____

_____

_____

_____

_____

_____

_____

_____

_____

_____

_____

_____

_____

Giving

Be willing to give, but do not give what you do not have. You don't necessarily have to give money; you can donate your time or resources, too. If a close friend or family member asks you if they can borrow money, and you don't have it to offer, do not run to the debit machine to pull out cash. It's unfortunate that the person is in their financial predicament, but you cannot be everyone's ATM. That is how you dig yourself into a financial hole. Sometimes you just have to say "No!"

Earlier in the book, we discussed the importance of saving 10 percent of your income; I like to give back 10 percent as well. I give to my local church and donate clothing and household items to my local Salvation Army and Goodwill stores. I also volunteer at my daughter's school and at my church. We all have our own ways of giving; however, it is up to you to decide what you want to give, how much you want to give, and to whom you want to give it.

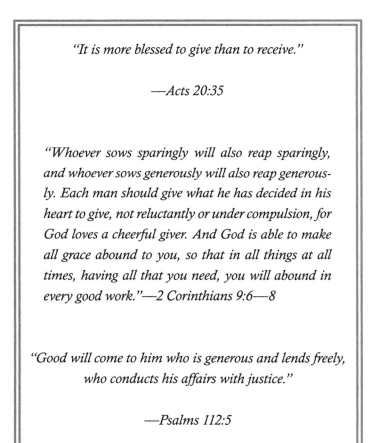

"It is more blessed to give than to receive."

—Acts 20:35

"Whoever sows sparingly will also reap sparingly, and whoever sows generously will also reap generously. Each man should give what he has decided in his heart to give, not reluctantly or under compulsion, for God loves a cheerful giver. And God is able to make all grace abound to you, so that in all things at all times, having all that you need, you will abound in every good work."—2 Corinthians 9:6—8

"Good will come to him who is generous and lends freely, who conducts his affairs with justice."

—Psalms 112:5

Consider whether you are giving too much or too little. If adjustments are necessary, list your solutions here:

_____

_____

_____

_____

_____

_____

_____

_____

_____

_____

_____

_____

_____

_____

_____

_____

_____

Second-Hand Stores

You've heard the saying, "Don't judge a book by its cover," right? Well, that applies to second-hand goods too, like those found at the Salvation Army, antique stores, or even yard sales. Sometimes you can find really nice items for an even nicer price.

When I was in the market for a desk and a television stand about two years ago, I went to my local Salvation Army during my lunch hour and browsed the store to see if there was anything I could use. To my surprise I found everything I needed for only $20. Now tell me that wasn't a good deal.

Before I purchase an item at retail price, I'll quickly check out the second-hand stores in the area. After all, the desk and television stand purchase saved me at least $80.

Make a list of items you currently need, with a star next to the items that could be found at your local second-hand store:

_____

_____

_____

_____

_____

_____

_____

_____

_____

_____

_____

_____

_____

_____

_____

_____

_____

Spiritual Wealth

There is more to life than physical wealth. Spiritual wealth is equally important so that you can live your life in fulfillment of the purpose for which you were created. To get out of a financial and mental rut, you have to modify your attitude as well as your actions—how you think about money, how you handle your finances, and how you learn from mistakes.

Spiritual wealth is something we all need; however, a lot of us may suffer from malnutrition.

> *"Man does not live by bread alone, but man lives by every word that comes from the mouth of the LORD."*
>
> *—Deuteronomy 8:3*

In addition to going to church weekly and reading my Bible, I signed up for spiritual food on www.JoelOsteen.com. On a daily basis, I receive an inspirational quote and interpretative explanation via e-mail. As I sit down at my desk to begin my day, I read my daily word, and feed my spirit with every message.

- Most of us nowadays have some kind of electronic device with more than enough applications. Why not download something that will stimulate your spirit?

- Whether you download an inspirational text or simply read a book, feed your spirit so that it stays healthy. A healthy spirit leads to an alert mind—which is better able to produce wealthy ideas.

It is important to manage your thoughts and maintain your focus. Whatever we focus on is what will be brought to light. So if you notice that you continue to focus on your lack of money or the bills that need to be paid, then you'll ultimately create more bills and less money. Instead, focus on how you are going to create more money, or on your gratitude for the positive things in your life. As you do this you will minimize the negativity, increase the positivity, and ultimately nourish your spiritual wealth.

> *You have to choose between thoughts that rob you of your drive and those that motivate you to take action.*

Write down steps you can take to improve your spiritual wealth:

_____

_____

_____

_____

_____

Reflect on how your spiritual well-being can produce financial gain; list your ideas here:

_____

_____

_____

_____

_____

_____

Taxes

If you had to pay the IRS or your state government during last year's tax season, you likely are not having enough taxes taken out of your regular paycheck. I know, I know, you feel like you are giving Uncle Sam enough of your money. But it's financially better to pay enough during the year so that you do not have to pay a large amount by April 15—especially if by then you don't have the money saved up to pay the amount owed. If that were to happen, you would have to arrange to make payments in addition to paying the inevitable penalties and interest charges. To adjust your taxation amounts, fill out a W-4 form from the IRS and the appropriate state form from your local taxing authority or human resources department, where you can also get assistance regarding your withholding changes. Once your form is complete you can submit it to your employer.

If you're a small business owner or plan on itemizing deductions, consider the following:

- Save your receipts. You may have more to write off than you realize. I tell my tax clients to keep an envelope in the door of their car and possibly in their office or bedroom. That way, you have a common and convenient place to store them, instead of throwing them away.

- Keep track of deductions and credits. If you are not sure what is tax-deductible, this can easily be done by simply holding on to every one of your receipts.

- Pay attention to tax law changes, as they may affect you negatively or positively. The most current information pertaining to tax laws can be found on www.irs.gov.

Now that you have your receipts and are prepared for your taxes, let's discuss what you can do with your refunds. I have several clients who use their anticipated tax refunds as an indirect savings method (meaning they're not necessarily saving monies on their own, there is just the anticipation of a tax refund check); for those that do this, let's discuss some of the ways to make the most of your refund.

- Pay off your debt, beginning with any outstanding high interest-bearing credit cards.

- Save it in an interest-bearing savings account; this could also serve as your emergency fund.

- Put additional monies towards the principal balance of your home. If done on a consistent basis, you can pay off your home sooner.

- Establish or fund a retirement or college savings account.

- After searching for the best deal, use some of the money to go on a vacation without using a credit card.

- Use your refund to generate more money. (Refer back to the Creating Income chapter for a review of your options.)

Whatever you decide to do with your tax refund, be frugal in your choices. Do not blow the money just because it's there. Use it wisely, and it will work hard for you.

> *When we consciously arrange our thoughts, we set ourselves up for success.*

What will you do with your next tax refund? Jot down your ideas here:

_____

_____

_____

_____

_____

_____

_____

_____

_____

_____

_____

_____

_____

_____

_____

_____

Organization

Whether it involves our life, our finances, or our health, it's essential to be organized so that we can make well-informed decisions. Plan your life; don't let it plan you. When you are overbooked, your bills are late, or you can't find your keys, use these tips to avoid a breaking point:

- Use a planner to schedule events and to keep track of tasks, to-do lists, and appointments.

- Go to a secluded place like a bedroom, a library, or a park. Just make sure it is a place where you will not be interrupted.

- Sit and think about what exactly it is that you want.

- Identify these items or goals and write them down.

- Consider your list once you are done and re-group items based on their importance to you.

- Next, visualize yourself achieving these goals. Once you feel as though you have accomplished them all, write out the steps you will take to get there.

- Avoid thoughts like "I don't know how." Instead, visualize what you want to take place.

- Identify what you do know is needed to accomplish your goal and research to find out more information on the areas that are unfamiliar.

- Pray for guidance and wisdom.

- Do not be afraid to ask for help.

Life can sweep you off your feet if you're not grounded. But before you can be grounded, you need to be organized. When you are organized, you are in control.

Write down the steps you will take to become better organized:

_____

_____

_____

_____

_____

_____

_____

_____

_____

_____

_____

_____

_____

_____

_____

_____

Travel

Have you ever come back from vacation, tallied your expenses, and thought, "I spent *that* much money?" Well, if you totaled your expenditures in the first place, you are in a better position than most. The majority of people don't track their expenses at all—they just know there is no money left at the end of their trip. Do not let this be you.

Here are some quick tips to consider when preparing to travel:

- Unless it is unavoidable, do not travel at the last minute. You'll get the best deals if you plan ahead. Identify when you're going to go, the location, how you'll get there, and who you'll take with you.

- Determine how much you can comfortably spend on your trip, and stay within your set guidelines.

- Use the Internet to find the best deals. (Refer back to the Shopping chapter for tips.)

- Avoid impulse buying when it comes to online travel purchases. For example, if you find yourself saying, "I have to buy this now, because they are going to run out," remember that in most cases there is more of whatever you are trying to purchase. Advertisements threatening low stock are usually just a marketing technique to get you to "Buy Now!" instead of buying later and from somewhere else.

- Consider saving money for a vacation on a monthly basis, so that you can take that dream trip in twelve months without using your charge card.

- If your trip requires that you park your car at the airport, pre-purchase your Park 'N Fly tickets. When my family and I took a week-long vacation in 2010, we pre-purchased the Park 'N Fly tickets from AAA.com for $48; if we had paid after our trip, we would have spent $91. I do have a AAA membership; however, my membership was not necessary at the time of purchase.

Plan ahead as much as possible to take advantage of discounts. Many littles make a lot. Many little discounts can cause a lot of money to be saved.

Planning a vacation? Make a list of ways you can save on travel expenses:

_____

_____

_____

_____

_____

_____

_____

_____

_____

_____

_____

Splurges

You're not a horrible person if you splurge on a pair of shoes that you have been wanting for several months. The problem comes if you splurge every time you receive a paycheck. The key is to be mindful of your spending habits. One of my first major splurges was a pair of Beyoncé VIP concert tickets: I paid about $1200 for the pair. Despite the splurge, I was still mindful of my spending. I went against my will and did not purchase the meet-and-greet tickets, priced at about $1200 *each*.

I cannot put into words how much I wanted to meet Beyoncé; she remains my all-time favorite entertainer. When her music came out, I could completely relate to the songs she sang and the feeling that was relayed through her music. To me she signifies beauty, strength, and a solid Christian upbringing, which is exactly how I feel about myself. I really do hope and pray that one day I get to meet

Beyoncé and work with her. More specifically, I would love to dance with her. However, when making that decision, I had to ask myself if I was willing to spend that much money given my other financial obligations. Ultimately, I decided it was best to practice self-control and maintain my financial health.

Here are some tips to help you fight the urge to splurge, too:

- Don't let one splurge turn into an excuse to overspend.

- Save up your money for that splurge. Sacrifice is an inevitable part of getting what we want.

- Always be mindful of your purchases.

- Take the time to think about your purchases before making them.

- Ask yourself how your financial needs will be affected if you make your purchase. In other words, will all your bills be paid even if you buy this item now?

> *Just like the saying, "Think before you speak," think before you buy!*

Identify some of your most recent splurges. How could you have handled those splurges differently?

_____

_____

_____

_____

_____

_____

_____

_____

_____

_____

_____

_____

_____

_____

_____

_____

_____

Most Common Financial Mistakes

We have to realize that we are human; sometimes we make bad financial choices and lose our good credit as a result, if not our house or job. Although it may feel like it is the end of the world at the time, I am a firm believer that when one door closes, God will surely open up another.

Here are some useful Dos and Don'ts:

Do:

- Realize what led you to this mistake.
- Admit your mistake.
- Ask someone you trust for help.
- Focus on the positive.
- Change the situation.
- Avoid making the same mistake again.
- Keep one of your credit cards, preferably one with a low interest rate, for emergency purpos-

es and online transactions—and get rid of the rest. (For online transactions, it's best to use a credit card instead of a check card attached to your bank account. Should your banking information get into the wrong hands, it could interfere with everyday needs. For example, if you're a victim of identity theft and need groceries while you are waiting for your bank to send you another check card, you would have to make an extra trip to the bank in order to make your purchase. However, if your credit card number was stolen, you would still have access to your money while you wait for a reissued credit card.)

Don't:

- Beat yourself up.
- Go and spend more.
- Level the spending binge with an eating binge.
- Complain about the situation—focus instead on preventing it from happening again.

Write down a few of your past financial mistakes, and what you will do to prevent similar mistakes from happening in the future:

Education Expenses

When I went to college, I thought my tuition was extremely expensive. Now, college is two, maybe three, times more expensive than it was back then. The financing for a four-year degree has changed so drastically that it is imperative to properly plan for this expense as early as possible. I have two young children who I plan to send to college, and since I have first-hand knowledge of the cost of schooling, I know how important it is to begin saving years in advance.

- Research alternatives to borrowing. Start exploring scholarships and grants to reduce the need for loans while the college-bound student is in high school. Fastweb.com is a good place to start.

- Be selective about the school of choice. Consider the school's affordability, location, and available course programs.

- Be conservative with the amount you are willing to borrow, and mindful of the amount you can afford to pay back.

- If it's not too late, start saving now for your future college-bound student's education.

- Make sure that you and your future student are aware of the costs associated with going to college and the importance of repaying the loan.

- Use the resources that are available to you, such as the following websites:

  Studentaid.ed.gov
  FinAid.org
  Collegeboard.com

- Take advantage of the 529 savings plan. This plan allows you to save money that is then tax-exempt; however, the funds must be used for education expenses.

Write down a few of your own cost-saving ideas regarding educational expenses:

_____

_____

_____

_____

_____

_____

_____

If applicable, write down how you plan on funding or saving for you or your dependents' educational expenses:

_____

_____

_____

_____

_____

_____

_____

Health & Beauty for Less

When it comes to health and beauty, do not be deceived into thinking that more expensive products equal better quality. There are many reasonably-priced products that work just as well as the department store or designer versions. I personally have used store-brand and brand-name products and I actually like both types. However, if your goal is to save money, be selective and choose the less expensive product.

You'll also want to be aware of what you're getting for your money. For example, I have purchased a foundation from Avon that has a built-in primer and oil-absorbing feature, as well as a significantly more expensive brand-name foundation that has good coverage, but does not set as well, last as long, or have a built-in primer to keep my skin from shining. In this comparison, Avon is the better buy both in terms of getting multiple products in one and having a lower cost—both of which save me money.

I have also purchased store-brand oil blotting sheets and the brand name version. Given the price difference—$5 vs. $20—you'd expect a significant difference in results, too. But in my experience, these two items both succeed in removing the oil from your skin, while keeping your makeup intact. Save that extra $15 and put it into your savings account instead.

My typical Monday looks like this:

- 8:30 p.m. Sunday night—Yes, my typical day starts with preparation the night before. Before going to bed, I prepare the next day's lunch (so that I eat healthier and save money) and my gym bag, which consists of my work clothes and shower items.

- 4:00 a.m.—I wake up, brush my hair and teeth, put on my gym clothes, grab my bag and lunch, and head to the gym by 4:55 a.m.

- 5:30 a.m.—I work out on my own doing a mix of cardio and weight training or go to a step class.

- 6:50 a.m.—I arrive at work and put on my face. Then I am ready to see the day.

- 7:00 a.m.—I am at my desk, ready to go. As an accountant and internal auditor, I audit and crunch numbers for ten hours a day, Monday through Thursday.

- 5:30 p.m.—I run to the door, ready to go home.

- 6:20 p.m.—I feed my family; have a glass of wine; and, depending on the night, either take my daughter to her dance class or attend a dance class of my own.

- 7:00 p.m.—While my daughter is in her dance class, I relax in the car and enjoy the hour to myself. I'll listen to music, meditate, pray, or browse the Internet on my laptop.

- 8:30 p.m.—I kiss the kids goodnight, finish my glass of wine, talk to my husband, and prepare my gym bag and lunch for the next day.

- 10 p.m.—I go to sleep. (Note: It's probably best to get at least eight hours of sleep. My current weekday schedule does not permit it; however, I always make up for it on the weekends.)

Health is very important no matter what stage you are in life. Whether you are a beginner or a professional body-builder, the most important thing is taking that first step and then being consistent. If you think about health and beauty in terms of financial independence, it is important to be conscientious of the things we do, the items we buy, and the money we waste. I have made many erroneous purchases in the hopes of maintaining my health without sufficiently considering the cost. For example, I have purchased exercise equipment that could have been bought for less, ordered diet pills that didn't work, paid too much for skin cream, and caused myself unnecessary anxiety every time because I knew that I'd wasted money. Research your purchases, refrain from impulse buying, and use these tips to create a better, healthier, wealthier you:

- Create a schedule that works for you. As illustrated in my typical Monday timeline, the only time I have to work out on a consistent basis is in the morning. I have to wake up early, but I do it for my health and because I like how I feel when I am done: accomplished, healthy, and sexy.

- Stick to a fitness plan once you've structured one to fit your schedule.

- Be committed—it helps if you love what you're doing. I love to dance, so I attend a hip-hop dance class every Wednesday night.

- Make preparations the night before, as necessary. It's easier to start your day when you can check these items off your to-do list.

- Instead of running to the vending machine or spending an extra $5 a day at the cafeteria, pack a lunch along with healthy snacks. The reward? An annual savings of at least $1300. Remember, many littles make a lot!

- Use products that will compliment your skin and body. For example, if you have oily skin, then it's best to use products that are made for the oily skin type. If your skin or hair is really dry, then use moisturizers that are made to combat the dryness and to lock in the moisture. I have found that baby oil gel and Palmers Cocoa Butter are both great moisturizers for the skin.

- Eat ground turkey instead of beef and pork, and whole grain wheat products instead of white flour products.

- Incorporate more lean protein into your diet such as tuna in water, chicken breast, and low-sugar protein shakes.

- Include more fruits and vegetables in your diet.

- Do not buy unhealthy, heavily processed snacks.

- Review package labels when you shop.

MY STORY

When I was in the seventh grade, I had a life-altering incident. I stepped on the scale and it read 202 pounds—almost 60 pounds over my goal weight. I was devastated and insecure, but I knew change started with me. So, I did something about it.

- I began working out at home every day for at least thirty minutes.

- I didn't have weights or money for a gym, so I used my mom's copy of Richard Simmons's "Sweatin' to the Oldies" and power walked around my neighborhood.

- I reduced my serving sizes and stopped eating my mom's delicious homemade cinnamon rolls.

- I started drinking a lot of water and green tea.

- I started playing basketball.

I lost about forty-five pounds and slowly but surely, I felt better about myself and my health. In addition to cutting out unnecessary food items, I was saving a lot of money because I was analyzing every purchase. Young women around me told me that I was their role model. As my self-confidence grew, I wanted to accomplish more for myself. So, immediately after high school, I enrolled at DeVry University and earned my bachelor's degree in accounting at the age of twenty. Then, by the grace of God and the help of my mom, I managed to get a good job. Two years later, I went back to school to earn my master's degree in human resource management.

The decisions you make, good or bad, will directly influence your future. Make informed, conscientious choices.

Write down how you can maintain your health and beauty while maintaining your personal budget:

_____

_____

_____

_____

_____

_____

Sensuality on a Budget

Although not usually a topic that comes up during a financial discussion, sensuality is still an expense. Whether unwinding from a long day or taking time for intimacy, use all your senses and you'll be healthier *and* wealthier in no time.

1. **Hear**—When it's time to unwind, turn off the noise, whether it's the television, the kids, your spouse, or your own thoughts. Turn on some soothing or relaxing music, such as jazz.
2. **Smell**—Use aromatherapy, warm scented oils, light candles, or spray some perfume. I enjoy burning incense and lighting my sweet pea candles while taking a warm, soothing bath—the definition of relaxing.
3. **See**—I can't relax if my house is in disarray, so I make sure to keep it clean. If you have young chil-

dren, you may have a Ninja Turtle in the walkway, a potty seat in the middle of the floor, or a shoe in the middle of the hallway just waiting for you to trip. Once these are cleared away, you can focus on what or whom you prefer to see.

4. **Taste**—Whether it's white chocolate-covered strawberries and a bottle of wine or cherry-tasting massage oil, put your senses to work.

5. **Touch**—A simple touch, a hug, a rub, or a kiss can make one's heart be in sheer bliss.

- If you are single, enjoy your alone time; one day you may wish you had a little more time to spend by yourself.
- Enjoy life as it comes.
- To the married lovebirds, enjoy one another completely, because tomorrow is not guaranteed. Don't be so worried about tomorrow that you forget about today.
- The best part about sensuality? You don't need a lot of money to enjoy it. I have purchased the following items from discount stores:

Wine
Strawberries
Raspberry-flavored body oil
Incense and candles
A jazz instrumental CD

Do what makes your heart content, as long as you are not breaking the bank to do it.

> *Take care of your body, your health, and your wealth.*
> *Only you are responsible for you.*

Think of ways you can explore your sensuality while maintaining your budget:

_____

_____

_____

_____

_____

_____

_____

_____

_____

_____

_____

Wealth Tips for a Lifetime

The following are some tips to live by—I certainly do.

- ✓ Commit to saving at least ten percent of your income.

- ✓ Effectively manage your budget, debt, credit, savings, and tax obligations.

- ✓ Establish and follow a money management plan.

- ✓ Utilize estate planning and life insurance to pass wealth to future generations.

- ✓ Live within your means.

✓ Create an investment plan to accommodate your children's education as well as your retirement needs.

✓ Take advantage of education to maximize your income potential. You can do this by going back to school or studying something of interest to obtain supplemental income. (For example, you could learn how to become a notary.)

✓ Consider homeownership as a basis for building wealth.

✓ Give to your church and your community, even if you just donate your time.

Write down tips you have learned that you can begin practicing today:

_____

_____

_____

_____

_____

_____

_____

How will you use these tips?

_____

_____

_____

_____

_____

_____

_____

_____

_____

_____

_____

_____

_____

_____

_____

_____

_____

Closing Thoughts

"Don't worry about anything; instead,
pray about everything. Tell God what you need,
and thank Him for all He has done."

—Philippians 4:6

- Always have an attitude of gratitude.
- Love yourself.
- Take time for you.
- Be a good saver.
- Be a cheerful giver.
- Be conscientious of your spending.
- Live your life with clarity; know where you are going.
- Think happy thoughts to attract happiness in your life.

Appendix

Strong to Be the Me That I Am

Positive Affirmations

Your Personal Notes & Sample Budget Worksheet

References

Strong to Be the Me That I Am

Oh Lord, when is my time, for the manifestation of my heart's desires. All my hopes and all my dreams are passionately burning inside of me like a brush fire.

I feel like I'm on the brink, of complete and total realization. But as I gasp for air, while catching my breath, I see it is not yet time for culmination.

Fetish for fun, Fetish for fight, Fetish for complete infamousness. Live for today, strive for tomorrow, and believing that I have reached all my goals, is the business.

What others feel about me is not my concern for me to surrender. What I think, feel, and believe about myself is ultimately what will be delivered.

Be true to thy self, and walk with your ambiance utterly focused and at ease. The epitome of unshaken self-worth will cause hope for others and your heart to be pleased.

As I pursue my tomorrow with sharp, astute precision, I want you to know as I-know-that-I-know, that you can accomplish anything in your life as long as you make a firm committed decision.

Strong, yes I am, this person I am. To love, to hold, this wonderful person I am.

A gift of life, from the King up above; despite what goes on he ensures I know that I'm loved.

Positive Affirmations

When spoken daily, affirmations can positively alter your mindset and change your way of life. A few of my favorites:

- I live in abundance.
- Everything I need and want comes to me.
- I have more than I need or desire.
- My bank accounts are overflowing with more than enough.
- I welcome, am open to, and receive all abundance that comes.
- I draw abundance to myself today and every day.
- Everything I do is a success.
- I am loving, understanding, and compassionate.
- I am very blessed to work at what I love to do.

- I have powerful and enjoyable business relationships.
- I am a strong and confident person.
- I only attract positive people into my life.
- I am loyal, smart, caring, and fun to be with.
- The past does not affect my future.
- I deserve all good things in my life.
- I am a winner.
- I am glowing with wealth and health.
- I am in, and deserve to be in, perfect health.
- I do not live over my means.
- I am rich and deserve to be rich.
- I enjoy exercising.
- I am worthy as a person.
- I am successful.
- I do not waste money.
- I am an abundant person.
- I enjoy creating wealth for me and my family.
- Success comes to me effortlessly.
- I am beautiful.
- I am a good saver of money.
- I am the lender and not the borrower.
- It is easy for me to save money and create wealth.

Write down some of your own positive affirmations:

_____

_____

_____

_____

_____

_____

_____

_____

_____

_____

_____

_____

_____

_____

_____

_____

_____

Your Personal Notes &
Sample Budget Worksheet

Notes:

SAMPLE BUDGET WORKSHEET (a tool to help manage your monthly expenses)				Notes:
Category	**Monthly Budget Amount**	**Actual Amount**	**Difference**	
INCOME:				
Wages/Income				
Interest Income				
INCOME SUBTOTAL				
EXPENSES:				
Taxes				
Rent/Mortgage				
Utilities				
Groceries/Food				
Clothing				
Shopping				
Entertainment				
Miscellaneous/Other				
Savings/Investments				
EXPENSES SUBTOTAL				
NET INCOME (Income - Expenses)				

References

The Lockman Foundation, *New American Standard Bible.* Anaheim: Foundations Publication, 1995.

About the Author

REBECCA SCOTT YOUNG is a senior internal accountant, auditor, and investment advisor. Having earned her MBA in human resource management from LaSierra University and her BA in accounting from DeVry University, she manages her own financial and tax services business from home. Currently working on a doctorate degree with an emphasis in entrepreneurship and business management at California InterContinental University, she lives in Moreno Valley, California with her husband and children.